ONE Question a DAY

to Stay
CLOSE &
CURIOUS

A Couple's Journal for a Lifetime of Love

GINA SENARIGHI, PhD, CPC

ZEITGEIST • NEW YORK

*To the thousands of clients who
have generously opened
their hearts with me*

Published in the United States by Zeitgeist, an imprint of Zeitgeist™,
a division of Penguin Random House LLC, New York.
zeitgeistpublishing.com

Zeitgeist™ is a trademark of Penguin Random House LLC
ISBN: 9780593689998

Cover art by © yugoro/Getty Images
Interior art by © Sunward Art/Shutterstock.com
Cover design by Katy Brown
Interior design by Erin Yeung
Author photograph © by Miriam Bulcher
Edited by Erin Nelson

Manufactured in China

1st Printing

Contents

Introduction

Every Friday for 10 years I sent five conversation prompts to more than 20,000 readers to nourish intimacy between partners. I started this practice because I saw so many couples longing for deeper connection in their relationships. Nearly all of them started as playful lovers filled with fascination for each other. They would stay up all night talking. But their intrigue had faded over time. They were a little bored and a lot disconnected.

Across the field of couples therapy, we have seen that those who have a regular, reliable practice of being present with each other last longer and report greater relationship satisfaction than those who don't actively participate in their togetherness. The research shows us that couples who stay curious about each other, engage in learning about each other, and are open to growing together will thrive more long-term. So, as a couples therapist, I encouraged my clients to create a daily ritual of connection, to set aside time to be together.

Like those questions from 10 years ago, the questions here are meant to inspire deeper sharing than the usual "How was your day?" exchange. I have heard over and over that the simple practice of sitting down with a partner and getting curious saved multiple relationships.

The more familiar you are with each other's inner worlds, the better you will fare through conflict and unexpected life changes. Couples who stay open-minded can better adapt to changes and navigate bumps in the road with resilience.

The bottom line is that staying close to your person means staying curious about them over time. Here are a few ways to keep curiosity alive:

* Allow yourself space to wonder. What could be going on in their mind?

* Check your assumptions about your partner. You might not know everything about them—and that's a good thing!

* Ask them meaningful questions. Take time to think about what you want to know about them and what you think they'd like to share with you.

* Fully listen to the response you get without responding immediately. If judgment arises, catch yourself—bring yourself back to that mindset of curiosity.

* Resist the urge to fix, teach, or scold. Again, this is about curiosity. There is a time and a place for tough conversations. The goal here is to create a comfortable—and fun—place to share.

* Ask follow-up questions for deeper understanding. This is how you keep the conversation alive!

How to Use This Journal

There are 150 questions inside this journal. That's five months' worth of solid curiosity, connection, and bonding if you choose to do one question a day, consecutively. Each page has space for you and your partner to write (above and below the line). Feel free to answer the question, doodle, leave love notes if you feel so inclined. Unlined space is there to support your unbridled creativity and love.

There is no right or wrong way to use the journal. You can flip through and choose what speaks to you that day or go in chronological order. To begin building your ritual of connection, find a time when you can set aside all other distractions and be fully present with your love for 10 to 30 minutes. Then commit to prioritizing your ritual. Don't let other things get in the way of it. This is hard. But keeping your love aflame means putting it above other responsibilities.

You can weave these questions into your practice in several ways. First, decide if this journal will be shared between you (in which case you may want notebooks to write in separately), or if you plan to each have a copy to be able to write and read responses to each other.

I always recommend couples set an intention for their practice or ritual. Your intention is your hopeful outcome for the practice (e.g., connection, understanding, peace, etc.). What's most important is that the two of you identify and share your intentions with each other, then keep them nearby. If you get stuck or find it hard to stay present, you'll have a reminder of your shared intention at hand.

Intention (Partner 1): _____

_____

Intention (Partner 2): _____

_____

I have seen couples adapt this writing ritual in several successful ways over the years. If you're not sure where to start, you might try different methods and see what you enjoy the most, or switch things up depending on the mood or situation.

Some of these questions have built-in follow-up questions. Feel free to incorporate them in your answers or skip them if you'd like to stick to one question. Although you might fill this journal in the coming months or year, keep ahold of these questions. As time goes on and seasons change, part of the fun is seeing how your answers evolve.

Below are a few ways I suggest using this journal. No matter what method(s) you choose, the prompts in the following pages can serve as a starting place for you to develop your own unique ritual of connection. As always, feel free to iterate along the way.

Share Space, Write, and Talk Together

Write down your answers—your stories—together. Once you're finished writing, you can pass your writing along to your partner to read or take turns sharing aloud. You can also use the questions as verbal prompts if you prefer a more rapid back-and-forth.

Write Solo, Share Together

Take turns writing down your answer to one of the questions on your own time, then come together to share with each other. When it's your turn to share, you'll read aloud and be open to follow-up questions from your partner. If you are the one listening, you'll want to focus your attention on really hearing and fully understanding your partner. Use this as your opening to validate, empathize, and ask more questions to grasp the nuances of your partner's experience.

Write Solo, Read Solo

Pass the book back and forth to write *and* read on your own time. This could mean leaving the journal in a special place for your partner to find or flagging certain questions you'd like them to answer. This method, more than any other, plays on a sense of excitement from anticipation. If you do choose this method, be sure to set aside time to come together to discuss what you learned and to deepen your conversations.

Let's Play

Turn the journal into a game: One person can circle two questions they'd like their partner to answer. The partner chooses one of those questions to answer. Write on your own time, write together, or share verbally. Note: There should always be agency for the storyteller; this is an important aspect of getting your partner to open up.

Tools to Support Loving Connection

Over the years, I've seen couples get stuck in two ways when beginning to work through these questions. For some, prompts related to early life can bring up undesirable memories. If you notice you or your partner struggling to think about earlier experiences, adjust the questions to other time frames or skip them entirely. Great moments of trust and trauma healing can come from couples staying present for each other and deciding to opt out of situations together. Stay connected in the moment and come back to a different question at another time.

I've also worked with couples who come to tools like these when they are deep in conflict and pain. In these cases, it's often best to respond with pure reflections of what your partner shares instead of adding assumptions or interpretations. The *Write Solo, Read Solo* method might be a good place for these couples to start.

The tools herewith will help you assess your strengths, get playful, appreciate each other, and support your relationship's health well into the future. The bottom line: If you really want to make the most of sharing, do your best to keep defensiveness, judgment, fixing, or critique as far from your ritual as possible. Any of those will block the two of you from the kind of vulnerability required for authentic connection.

I hope these prompts help you connect in meaningful ways with the person you love. Here are some tips to help you make the most of this book.

Tip #1: Be Present

Set aside some fully present, distraction-free time to ask and respond to these questions with the person you love. Put down your phone, walk away from any screens, and give your partner your full attention.

Tip #2: Stay Open to Possibility

Even if you think you know your partner's responses, listen to them without assumption so they have room to surprise you.

Tip #3: Follow Up

Part of this process is about engaging with your partner in meaningful ways. Asking follow-up questions—in the moment or later—will show that you care and broaden the conversation.

Tip #4: Keep It Specific

Sharing specific answers helps your partner get to know you intimately. Try to remember details around certain memories, behaviors, or emotions.

Tip #5: Show Up

Offer responses in complete sentences, and challenge yourself to elaborate. This isn't about being brief—it's about growing a more meaningful connection.

Tip #6: Widen Your Connection

Take your questions on a date night, to a dinner party, or on a road trip to inspire deeper conversation with your community. Research shows that the more you experience your relationship in a positive light in the outside world, the more connected you'll feel at home.

Tip #7: Embrace the Changing Seasons

As the season changes, so do we, and therefore so does our relationship. If we don't stop to check in, we miss opportunities to celebrate, reconnect, and grow together with intention. I hope this journal inspires you to stay deeply connected through all of life's changing seasons.

Part 1

What Makes You, You?

The first half of this journal takes you back to the basics. What shaped you and your partner into the people you are today? What are your hopes, fears, and greatest desires? When do you each feel most like (or unlike) yourselves? These chapters will weave you through a journey of your inner workings.

CHAPTER 1

The Truest You

I start with this list because it gets to the root of what couples want to know about each other. After more than a decade of helping couples deepen their bond, these are the areas that appear again and again. Use the following questions to jump into who you each are, and what makes you tick. Remember, even if you think you know everything about your partner, uncovering new details from their life—and sharing stories from your own—will help you stay closer over time.

What's one thing—even a tiny thing—that's
going well in your life right now?

What's the story of your most treasured possession?

Tell me about a time you got lost.
How did you eventually find your way?

What do you wish you had more
room for in your daily life?

When was the last time you were fully
immersed in what you were doing?

Share one event that changed your life.
What did you learn from it?

What is one thing you wish you could get closure on?
What would that closure look like?

What helps you feel refreshed and renewed?

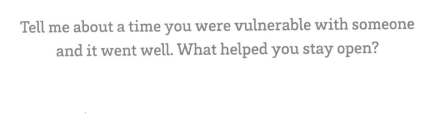

Tell me about a time you were vulnerable with someone and it went well. What helped you stay open?

Who is someone you admire
at this stage in your life? Why?

What's the biggest risk you've ever taken?

Do you believe in regrets?

When was the hardest you ever laughed?

Have any of your fears softened over time?

When was the last time you felt completely surprised?

Tell me about one of the best presents you ever received. Why is it different from other gifts?

Tell me about a time you cried tears of joy.
How does that memory make you feel now?

What's a place you visited that left
a lasting impression on you?

Tell me about a time you were deeply confused.
How did you resolve your confusion?

_____

What is the worst life advice you've ever received?
What do you wish the advice had been instead?

When do you feel most proud of yourself?

When do you feel most alive?

CHAPTER 2

Your Values in Action

Disconnect is often caused by a misunderstanding of different core values and how those values appear in day-to-day life. As you engage with the following questions, remember your partner's values are key to understanding and loving them well. Challenge yourself to be honest as you share, and openhearted as you learn more about your love's values in action.

What is the best compliment you've ever received?
What made it special to you?

When was the first time you remember witnessing or experiencing someone else's generosity?

What's the most generous thing you've ever done?

What does healthy communication look like to you right now? How do you know when it's been achieved?

_____

What usually sparks disappointment for you?

Which of your core values most
dictates your daily actions?

What does community mean to you?

Which holiday feels most meaningful to
you and why? What actions or celebrations
help you connect with that meaning?

What role does community engagement play
in your life? Is there a particular movement
or cause that resonates with you?

Do you consider yourself a rule follower?

What lesson do you wish more people in
the world understood and lived by?

What do you hope people say about you?

CHAPTER 3

Feeling Your Feelings

Couples often ask how they can expand their emotional intimacy—to feel as close as they did in those magical early days. Relearning how to hold space for your partner's emotions is the first step to building this emotional intimacy. These questions can help you get back on that path.

If your emotional landscape were a weather report for today, what would the meteorologist say?

Which three emotions do you want to
feel most and why?

What emotion is hardest for you to express?

When was the last time you felt bored?
When did you start feeling engaged again?

When was a time you were so excited
you couldn't sit still or sleep?

When do you feel most confident?

What pulls you out of a dark day?

When did you last feel nervous?

When was the last time you felt a sense of awe?

Where are you experiencing the most
satisfaction in life right now?

When was the last time you felt a sense of awe?

Where do you currently turn to for inspiration?

What gives you hope?

Tell me about a time you felt invincible.
What helped you feel so courageous?

CHAPTER 4

Little You,
Big You

Our early-life experiences lay a foundation for lifelong relationships, but it's easy to lose sight of the ways our early life impacts us today. While many of these questions evoke playfulness and fun, they can also bring up big feelings. Remember, you always have the option to skip what doesn't serve you.

What was your biggest dream as a child?

What's an unforgettable memory
from your childhood summers?

_____

What band or music heavily influenced
your teen years?

What do you appreciate most
about where you grew up?

_____

What did you learn about feelings in your early life?

What did your childhood
teach you about trust?

Growing up, what did it mean to "have enough"
or "not have enough"? What morals
did these messages instill?

How did your family react
when you made mistakes?

What power dynamics from your childhood
have become clearer with age?

What did you learn about forgiveness as a young person? Have those lessons changed over time?

Do you ever experience nostalgia?

What influential figure did you most admire
when you were growing up?

What did your early-life experiences
teach you about gender roles?

How is your dream home like or unlike
the home you grew up in?

_____

CHAPTER 5

Your Life's Work (So Far)

Try using the following questions to better understand how your partner spends their day. This is an opportunity to learn and share around what evokes frustration and purpose, hope and longing. We are what we feel, and also what we do.

What would your day look like if it were more closely aligned with your passions?

When is it easiest for you to have an open mind?

What problem are you most interested
in solving right now?

What's one responsibility you
wish you could off-load?

Take two minutes to vent about work—whatever
that entails for you. Have at it!

What's something you *don't* want your coworkers to know about you? What's something you wish they knew?

Describe what you think I do for a living.
What do you think my dream job is?

_____

When was the last time you felt inspired at work?

When do you find it
easiest to receive praise?

What legacy do you hope to leave behind
with the work that you do?

Tell me how you discovered one of your strengths on the job. How has this strength grown?

What motivates you to show up each day?

CHAPTER 6

All About Love

We talk about love like it is a singular destination, but love that lasts a lifetime takes many pit stops and detours as it makes new discoveries and redefines itself. Even on the same journey, each of us experiences love a little bit differently. Play around with these questions to explore the ways you and your partner view and experience love. This is an important step in expanding the love you share.

Tell me about a time when you felt incredibly loved.
How was it shown to you?

How is a relationship different from friendship?

What are some of the most exciting parts
of dating (or being married) for you?

How would you define love to a child?

_____

What romantic advice would you
give yourself 10 years ago?

What is the best relationship advice
you've ever received?

_____

Tell me about the best meal you've ever had.
How could I re-create it for you?

How do you know when you love someone?

What does meaningful support look
like in a romantic relationship?

What does love look like on an ordinary day?

What Makes Us, Us?

The most recent research on couples' lasting wellness shows us that couples who nourish their bond with gratitude, appreciation, and affection report higher overall relationship and life satisfaction. Here you will delve into who you are within the context of each other.

CHAPTER 7

All About Us

One secret to invigorating your love is to relive the parts that make it special. Many relationship experts say that couples who recall their meet-cute or origin story in a positive way are more likely to enjoy their current relationship. The questions in this section are here for you to celebrate the great joys you've shared and honor (with a little humor) your ongoing connection. They also give you the chance to explore those which you are actively writing. Enjoy this time of reminiscing as you write the next chapter of your story.

When was the moment you knew
you were in love with me?

When do you think I fell in love with you?

What told you I loved you other than my words?

When was a moment you felt proud to be with me?

What is one of our greatest
accomplishments as a couple?

_____

If you were to write a book about our relationship so far, what would the title be?

What have you learned from me in this partnership?

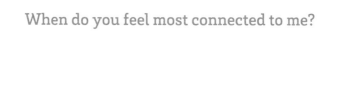

When do you feel most connected to me?

When do you feel most loved by me? Which loving behaviors carry the most meaning for you?

What's one thing you feel like I
really understand about you?

What do I do to help make your life easier?

In what ways do you feel we are most compatible?

What makes you feel respected in our partnership?

What's the greatest way we've ever celebrated us?

What is unique about our partnership?

What three words would you use
to sum up our relationship?

Is there anything I've convinced you to do or like that you thought you never would?

_____

What's something we do that other people might find weird but that you find endearing?

When did we do something outside
of your comfort zone?

What do you wish we could do more of together?

What skills do we have that could
help us survive an apocalypse?

When was a time you felt like we were on the same
team? Bonus: What would our mascot have been?

If we had a relationship bucket list, what
would some of the top items be?

What is one thing you hope
for us in the future?

CHAPTER 8

Building a Life Together

Building a life with a partner often doesn't come with enough discussion about what that life will look like, how it will evolve, and how it will make each person feel. The questions in this chapter are designed to help you think about the most important elements of your life in a new way and come to better understand what they mean to both you and your partner—no matter what stage of life you're in.

How do you want to feel when you
come home at the end of the day?

What is your favorite place in (y)our home?

_____

What reminds you of home?

What does family mean to you at
this point in your life?

When do you notice you feel most
secure in relationships?

Do you want to grow our family?
What does "growth" mean to you?

Are there any family traditions
you want to continue or create?

What do you envision (y)our family
looking like 10 years from now?

Where do you feel most supported outside of the home?

What's something you love to do alone? In what ways can I support you from a distance?

How has luck or good fortune played a role in your life?

What do you strive for? What drives your ambition?

What's one thing I can do to support
your personal growth?

Would you rather spend money on
things or experiences?

What is a secret passion you want to pursue?

CHAPTER 9

Our Physical Connection

It's normal to struggle to talk about physical intimacy; most people have a hard time with it. These questions were created to help you ease into talking about some of the most important and often overlooked aspects of physical connection between partners. As always, if a question doesn't resonate with you, skip it. Many of these questions can be applied to relationships and life in general.

When and how do you like to receive affection?

What might change if you allowed
more pleasure into your life?

When was a time you asked for something
and I was able to deliver?

What makes it easier for you
to connect with your body?

How has your self-confidence shifted
over time? How would you like to see it grow?

What's the first fantasy to pop into your mind?

How do you like to be seduced?

If our sex life were a dessert,
what would it be and why?

How is good sex different from great sex?

What does it mean to you to be sexually satisfied?

CHAPTER 10

Dreams and Imagination

I've worked with hundreds of couples who lose their ability to laugh and share dreams because they are too focused on the mundane aspects of their lives. Use these questions to get playful, embrace your creativity, and start dreaming together. Then, watch your desires turn into reality.

What is your favorite escape from daily life?

What animal are you most like? What about me?
How do we complement each other in the wild?

What's a vacation you've been dreaming about?
Walk me through the highlights.

You've just won the lottery—what's
the first thing we are doing?

We're a superhero team. What are our secret powers?

We are having a dinner party, and you can invite three people (dead or alive). Who are you inviting?

What romantic movie, book, or song
always makes you think of us?

_____

What is one dream you want to make
sure comes true in our lifetime?

CHAPTER 11

Looking Forward Together

Couples with a positive outlook and clear vision for their future fare better over time. You don't have to want the exact same things. But aligning your future is a good way to gather momentum around the things that will enrich your lives. These prompts are designed to inspire you to look forward to life down the road.

How do you hope our relationship grows this year?

What do you imagine us working
toward in the coming years?

If you woke up in the morning and our biggest worry
was resolved, what would change?

Which of your unique traits are you hoping
will or won't grow as you age?

What hobbies do you imagine we'll
have when we're older?

What does "aging well" mean to you?

What memory do you hope stands out
in our history together?

What's something you think will
always keep us young?

How do you want to be remembered as a couple?

References

Algoe, Sara B., Shelly L. Gable, and Natalya C. Maisel. "It's the Little Things: Everyday Gratitude as a Booster Shot for Romantic Relationships." *Personal Relationships* 17, no. 2 (June 2010): 217–33.

Gable, Shelly L., Gian C. Gonzaga, and Amy Strachman. "Will You Be There for Me When Things Go Right? Supportive Responses to Positive Event Disclosures." *Journal of Personality and Social Psychology* 91, no. 5 (November 2006): 904–17.

Holmberg, Diane, Kathryn M. Bell, and Kim Cadman. "Now for the Good News: Self-Perceived Positive Effects of the First Pandemic Wave on Romantic Relationships Outweigh the Negative." *Journal of Social and Personal Relationships* 39, no. 1 (January 2022): 34–55.

Other Great Books for Couples

Daring Greatly: How the Courage to Be Vulnerable Transforms the Way We Live, Love, Parent, and Lead by Brené Brown

Mating in Captivity: Reconciling the Erotic and the Domestic by Esther Perel

The Seven Principles for Making Marriage Work by John M. Gottman and Nan Silver

About the Author

Gina Senarighi, PhD, CPC, is a bestselling author, teacher, sexuality counselor, and award-winning relationship coach. She's been supporting happy, healthy relationships as a couples therapist and educator since 2009. Gina has written several books, cohosts the relationship podcast *Swoon*, and currently leads couples retreats coaching clients all over the world to have deeper intimacy and more meaningful communication. When she's not working, you'll find her in the garden with her two kids and partner, Rae.